LIVE BOLDLY

WORKBOOK

EPISODES 1-15

BY: NICKI CORINNE WHITE

LIVE BOLDLY

INTENTIONALLY
IN TODAY'S WORLD
WORKBOOK

Published by Carpenter's Son Publishing, Franklin, TN
Scripture quotations marked (NASB) are taken
from the New American Standard Bible,
Copyright © 1960, 1962, 1963, 1968, 1971, 1972,
1973, 1975, 1977, 1995 by The Lockman Foundation
Used by permission. (www.Lockman.org)
Front cover artwork by Nicki Corinne White
Interior design by Debbie Manning Sheppard
Printed in the United States of America

DEDICATION

Welcome to the Live Boldly Workbook! While workbooks generally do not have a dedication page, listing my contributors is important to me.

Five years ago, I attended a writers' conference and was encouraged to build a team. I wondered about this as I had not yet published a book. However, I already had someone take pictures and a few people had read and helped edit my manuscript. With others helping with my schedule and website, I realized I already had the start of a wonderful team.

Within the next month I had a publisher, book cover, press kit, release date, and book trailer. A year later I had book number two and a team of sixteen. The team blessedly continues to grow with the ministry needs.

Today, Live Boldly Ministries includes three books, a workbook, websites, video series, YouTube channel, social media outlets, and a compassion ministry resource.

This book is dedicated to my team, to those who began the journey with me five years ago and those who have joined me since. I could not do this without you and I thank the Lord for your desire to grow this ministry alongside me.

MY MINISTRY TEAM

- ❖ CRAIG WHITE - husband, tech support, video editor, graphics

- ❖ JESSICA EVERETT - daughter, executive administrator, scheduling, emails, editor, social media, marketing, basically everything

- ❖ NATHAN WHITE - son, websites, tech support

- ❖ MAUREEN LOEFFLER - editor, tech support, advisor

- ❖ JAMIE HUDSON - photographer, editor

- ❖ JESSICA OWINYO - creative consultant (genius), graphics, logos, social media

- ❖ RUTHANNE BEDDOE - editor, spiritual advisor

- ❖ TORI LOEFFLER - social media

- ❖ LISA SHUMAKER - sister, Col 3:12 Ministries team, marketing

- ❖ DEBBIE MERRITT - photographer, social media

- ❖ MARSHA PHILBROOK - editor

- ❖ ASHLEY TAYLOR - Col 3:12 Ministries team

- ❖ KAREN LAW - Col 3:12 Ministries team, libraries

- ❖ LINDA SARACOFF - photographer, social media

- ❖ JONI SULLIVAN BAKER - Buoyancy PR. She has encouraged me, been patient with me as a new author and been easy to approach with my many questions.

- ❖ Also my editor TAMMY KLING who gave me the great idea to do the video series and this workbook. She is a *worldchanger.*

TABLE OF CONTENTS

INTRODUCTION

INTRODUCTION

When Covid hit I was in the process of promoting my second book, *"It's Not About The Pie: A Fresh Look at Hospitality"*. I had just gone to a media conference and did several interviews for radio and TV, and a week later our state shutdown. A week after that, we had an earthquake. We all thought (little did we know) that everything would be fine in a couple weeks. But things just got worse, not to mention that our country had been polarized by a recent election. Things got worse and worse. People were wondering what was going to become of us all. They were nervous and had a fear of the unknown future. There is a famous quote by Corrie ten Boom you may have heard, "Never be afraid to trust an unknown future to a known God." And I kept thinking, people need God more than ever and HE IS STILL ON THE THRONE. God knows exactly what is happening; He is not surprised by any of this.

God wants us to continue to serve, continue to share His Word and to provide comfort. I put aside my other idea for a third book and thought about all the people out there serving God in dangerous places, or even just in their neighborhoods that were not stopping their ministry because of a pandemic. I knew this is what I needed to do. And so my third book, **"BOLD - Living Intentionally In Today's World"** was written. There are three sections:

I. Testimonies of people still living who are being BOLD for the gospel and sharing with others even when it is not easy.

II. Individuals no longer living who are heroes of faith, some giving their life for the gospel.

III. Examples from the Bible of those who stand out doing extraordinary things for God.

As that book was being published, my editor suggested that I do a video series titled: Live Boldly. I began doing a weekly video series which is why this workbook was developed - to expand your understanding of the information used in the videos. It can be used alongside the videos for your own personal study or with a Bible study group. I hope you enjoy this guide, pray it will encourage you to be intentional in your life of serving our great God, and hope it helps you to live boldly.

YouTube Channel: Nicki Corinne White

https://www.youtube.com/channel/UCaBhOM-9D7azX2REDRrDayMQ

Facebook Group: LIVE BOLDLY

https://www.facebook.com/groups/356149749641688

EPISODE 1

YOU TOO CAN DO THIS

Nehemiah 1-4

> 1 The words of Nehemiah the son of Hacaliah. Now it happened in the month Chislev, in the twentieth year, while I was in Susa the capitol, 2 that Hanani, one of my brothers, and some men from Judah came; and I asked them about the Jews who had escaped and had survived the captivity, and about Jerusalem. 3 And they said to me, "The remnant there in the province who survived the captivity are in great distress and disgrace, and the wall of Jerusalem is broken down and its gates have been burned with fire." 4 Now when I heard these words, I sat down and wept and mourned for days; and I was fasting and praying before the God of heaven. 5 I said, "Please, Lord God of heaven, the great and awesome God, who keeps the covenant and faithfulness for those who love Him and keep His commandments: 6 let Your ear now be attentive and Your eyes open, to hear the prayer of Your servant which I am praying before You now, day and night, on behalf of the

sons of Israel Your servants, confessing the sins of the sons of Israel which we have committed against You; I and my father's house have sinned. 7 We have acted very corruptly against You and have not kept the commandments, nor the statutes, nor the ordinances which You commanded Your servant Moses. 8 Remember, please, the word which You commanded Your servant Moses, saying, 'If you are unfaithful, I will scatter you among the peoples; 9 but if you return to Me and keep My commandments and do them, though those of you who have been scattered were in the most remote part of the heavens, I will gather them from there and bring them to the place where I have chosen to have My name dwell.' 10 They are Your servants and Your people whom You redeemed by Your great power and by Your strong hand. 11 Please, Lord, may Your ear be attentive to the prayer of Your servant and the prayer of Your servants who delight to revere Your name, and please make Your servant successful today and grant him mercy before this man." Now I was the cupbearer to the king.

This episode began by sharing a bit of background on my ministry and why I decided to begin these videos. I will briefly tell you that after a difficult childhood, death of my adoptive dad, no income, and wishing someone would help us, I became a person who was drawn to compassion ministries and that is why I wrote my first two books, "Not Really A Princess" and "It's Not About the Pie: A Fresh Look at

Hospitality." This workbook and video series is based on my third book, "Bold - Living Intentionally In Today's World." It is an in-depth study on believers growing in their faith and living their life with intention, and boldly living for God no matter the circumstances. Hopefully this workbook will encourage you as you grow in the knowledge of our Lord.

This episode also discusses how Nehemiah was saddened that the walls of Jerusalem were broken down. The Jewish people returned to Jerusalem after 70 years of captivity in Babylon as punishment for sin, and they rebuilt the temple but the city of Jerusalem's walls were in ruins.

Nehemiah encouraged the people to start building the wall around the city. They were just ordinary people and not necessarily masons or carpenters but had willing hearts. With faith, they built the wall!

Let's get this started.

QUESTIONS

1. *Do you sometimes feel inadequate to follow God's plan? Read Nehemiah chapter 1. Nehemiah reminds the Israelites that if they follow God and revere Him, God will give them the power to fulfill His plan. Do you have an example of this in your own life?*

_____

_____

_____

_____

2. *What verses help you when you feel overwhelmed and think you cannot accomplish what God directs you to do? Read 2 Chronicles 15:7; Psalm 33:11; Psalm 57:2. How do these verses encourage you?*

_____

_____

_____

_____

3. *What does God tell us about moving forward in our walk with Him? Read Philippians 3:13-14. These verses are my favorites on how to move forward even when the task seems impossible. We need to let go of our fears and have God direct us in our path. What do you need to forget about or let go of in order to move forward?*

_____

_____

_____

_____

_____

_____

_____

4. *Fix your eyes on Jesus. If our eyes are on ourselves we cannot move forward with His plan. Read Hebrews 12:1-2, which tells us to set aside what entangles us and to fix our eyes on Jesus. What do you need to set aside? Are your eyes on Jesus, or on someone or something else?*

_____

_____

_____

_____

5. *Read 1 Peter 4:7-11. Each of us has received a special gift. What gift do you have? How can you use it to serve others?*

_____

_____

_____

_____

6. *What purposeful step will you take this week that may be out of your comfort zone? How can you minister to someone near you this week?*

_____

_____

_____

_____

EPISODE 2

WHAT IS YOUR GOLIATH?

I Samuel 17

> **1** Now the Philistines gathered their armies for battle; and they were gathered at Socoh which belongs to Judah, and they camped between Socoh and Azekah, in Ephes-dammim. **2** Saul and the men of Israel were gathered and camped in the valley of Elah, and drew up in battle array to encounter the Philistines. **3** The Philistines stood on the mountain on one side while Israel stood on the mountain on the other side, with the valley between them. **4** Then a champion came out from the armies of the Philistines named Goliath, from Gath, whose height was six cubits and a span. **5** He had a bronze helmet on his head, and he was clothed with scale-armor which weighed five thousand shekels of bronze. **6** He also had bronze greaves on his legs and a bronze javelin slung between his shoulders. **7** The shaft of his spear was like a weaver's beam, and the head of his spear

weighed six hundred shekels of iron; his shield-carrier also walked before him. **8** *He stood and shouted to the ranks of Israel and said to them, "Why do you come out to draw up in battle array? Am I not the Philistine and you servants of Saul? Choose a man for yourselves and let him come down to me.* **9** *If he is able to fight with me and kill me, then we will become your servants; but if I prevail against him and kill him, then you shall become our servants and serve us."* **10** *Again the Philistine said, "I defy the ranks of Israel this day; give me a man that we may fight together."* **11** *When Saul and all Israel heard these words of the Philistine, they were dismayed and greatly afraid.* **12** *Now David was the son of the Ephrathite of Bethlehem in Judah, whose name was Jesse, and he had eight sons. And Jesse was old in the days of Saul, advanced in years among men.* **13** *The three older sons of Jesse had gone after Saul to the battle. And the names of his three sons who went to the battle were Eliab the firstborn, and the second to him Abinadab, and the third Shammah.* **14** *David was the youngest. Now the three oldest followed Saul,* **15** *but David went back and forth from Saul to tend his father's flock at Bethlehem.* **16** *The Philistine came forward morning and evening for forty days and took his stand.* **17** *Then Jesse said to David his son, "Take now for your brothers an ephah of this roasted grain and* *these ten loaves and run to the camp to your brothers. **18** Bring also these ten cuts of cheese to the commander of their thousand, and look into the welfare of your brothers, and bring back news of them. **19** For Saul and they and all the men of Israel are in the valley of Elah, fighting with the Philistines." **20** So David arose early in the morning and left the flock with a keeper and took the supplies and went as Jesse had commanded him. And he came to the circle of the camp while the army was going out in battle array shouting the war cry. **21** Israel and the Philistines drew up in battle array, army against army. **22** Then David left his baggage in the care of the baggage keeper, and ran to the battle line and entered in order to greet his brothers. **23** As he was talking with them, behold, the champion, the Philistine from Gath named Goliath, was coming up from the army of the Philistines, and he spoke these same words; and David heard them. **24** When all the men of Israel saw the man, they fled from him and were greatly afraid. **25** The men of Israel said, "Have you seen this man who is coming up? Surely he is coming up to defy Israel. And it will be that the king will enrich the man who kills him with great riches and will give him his daughter and make his father's house free in Israel." **26** Then David spoke to the men who were standing by him, saying, "What will be done for the man who kills* this Philistine and takes away the reproach from Israel? For who is this uncircumcised Philistine, that he should taunt the armies of the living God?" **27** The people answered him in accord with this word, saying, "Thus it will be done for the man who kills him." **28** Now Eliab his oldest brother heard when he spoke to the men; and Eliab's anger burned against David and he said, "Why have you come down? And with whom have you left those few sheep in the wilderness? I know your insolence and the wickedness of your heart; for you have come down in order to see the battle." **29** But David said, "What have I done now? Was it not just a question?" **30** Then he turned away from him to another and said the same thing; and the people answered the same thing as before. **31** When the words which David spoke were heard, they told them to Saul, and he sent for him. **32** David said to Saul, "Let no man's heart fail on account of him; your servant will go and fight with this Philistine." **33** Then Saul said to David, "You are not able to go against this Philistine to fight with him; for you are but a youth while he has been a warrior from his youth." **34** But David said to Saul, "Your servant was tending his father's sheep. When a lion or a bear came and took a lamb from the flock, **35** I went out after him and attacked him, and rescued it from his mouth; and when he rose up against me, I seized him by his

*beard and struck him and killed him. **36** Your*
servant has killed both the lion and the bear; and
this uncircumcised Philistine will be like one of
them, since he has taunted the armies of the living
*God." **37** And David said, "The Lord who delivered*
me from the paw of the lion and from the paw of the
bear, He will deliver me from the hand of this
Philistine." And Saul said to David, "Go, and may
*the Lord be with you." **38** Then Saul clothed David*
with his garments and put a bronze helmet on his
*head, and he clothed him with armor. **39** David*
girded his sword over his armor and tried to walk,
for he had not tested them. So David said to Saul, "I
cannot go with these, for I have not tested them."
*And David took them off. **40** He took his stick in his*
hand and chose for himself five smooth stones from
the brook, and put them in the shepherd's bag which
he had, even in his pouch, and his sling was in his
*hand; and he approached the Philistine. **41** Then the*
Philistine came on and approached David, with the
*shield-bearer in front of him. **42** When the Philistine*
looked and saw David, he disdained him; for he was
but a youth, and ruddy, with a handsome appear-
*ance. **43** The Philistine said to David, "Am I a dog,*
that you come to me with sticks?" And the Philis-
*tine cursed David by his gods. **44** The Philistine*
also said to David, "Come to me, and I will give
your flesh to the birds of the sky and the beasts of

*the field." **45** Then David said to the Philistine, "You come to me with a sword, a spear, and a javelin, but I come to you in the name of the Lord of hosts, the God of the armies of Israel, whom you have taunted. **46** This day the Lord will deliver you up into my hands, and I will strike you down and remove your head from you. And I will give the dead bodies of the army of the Philistines this day to the birds of the sky and the wild beasts of the earth, that all the earth may know that there is a God in Israel, **47** and that all this assembly may know that the Lord does not deliver by sword or by spear; for the battle is the Lord's and He will give you into our hands." **48** Then it happened when the Philistine rose and came and drew near to meet David, that David ran quickly toward the battle line to meet the Philistine. **49** And David put his hand into his bag and took from it a stone and slung it, and struck the Philistine on his forehead. And the stone sank into his forehead, so that he fell on his face to the ground. **50** Thus David prevailed over the Philistine with a sling and a stone, and he struck the Philistine and killed him; but there was no sword in David's hand. **51** Then David ran and stood over the Philistine and took his sword and drew it out of its sheath and killed him, and cut off his head with it. When the Philistines saw that their champion was dead, they fled. **52** The men of Israel and Judah arose and* *shouted and pursued the Philistines as far as the valley, and to the gates of Ekron. And the slain Philistines lay along the way to Shaaraim, even to Gath and Ekron. 53 The sons of Israel returned from chasing the Philistines and plundered their camps. 54 Then David took the Philistine's head and brought it to Jerusalem, but he put his weapons in his tent. 55 Now when Saul saw David going out against the Philistine, he said to Abner the commander of the army, "Abner, whose son is this young man?" And Abner said, "By your life, O king, I do not know." 56 The king said, "You inquire whose son the youth is." 57 So when David returned from killing the Philistine, Abner took him and brought him before Saul with the Philistine's head in his hand. 58 Saul said to him, "Whose son are you, young man?" And David answered, "I am the son of your servant Jesse the Bethlehemite."*

Is your **Goliath** a person you have put off talking with for a long time and you are tentative to approach? Or maybe it is a work project you don't know how to begin because it is too overwhelming? Perhaps it's that closet that needs sorting and cleaning before it will stay shut. We ALL have things in our life that we believe we can't possibly tackle. I have felt this way many times. As a matter of fact, I am a person who has a hard time focusing when I have a project I don't feel I can conquer. **So what do I do?**

I have found the best way for me to tackle my obstacle is to pray first, before I make it seem bigger than I can handle. I enlist help. Somehow I feel much better with someone to help ease the burden. Then I think of examples of others who had much bigger problems, and somehow I start feeling a bit better. Then I take one step at a time.

I admit that when I consider the Bible, one of the first examples that comes to mind is the young David fighting for his people and killing the giant Goliath. This is a well known story. However, you may not know all the details if you have not read the passage in your Bible. 1 Samuel 17 tells the story. The great warriors, the Philistines, wanted to take over the land. They had better weapons than Israel and an enormous army. They had an extremely large warrior fighting for them named Goliath. Historians believe he was about 9 feet tall, and he had metal armor covering his entire body.

Israel was scared. For 40 days, with Israel on one hill and the Philistines on another, the two armies faced off. The Philistines had proposed an arrangement. If Israel won the battle, then the Philistines would be their servants. If the Philistines won, then Israel would be their servants. No Israelite stepped forward to fight Goliath - until David arrived at the camp.

Prior to this, in 1 Samuel 16, God directed the prophet Samuel to go to a well- known man in the area to choose who would be king from amongst his sons. One by one he went to each son and declared that they were not the one chosen by God. Samuel finally asked, "Do you have any other sons?" The father told him that he had one more son who was young and out tending the sheep. Samuel told him to bring the boy to him. When he saw David, he knew that he was God's chosen.

When it was time to fight, David grabbed his sling and five smooth stones. The king of Israel wanted him to wear armor but David would not. He confronted Goliath and said, "You come to me with sword, a spear and a javelin, but I come to you in the name of the Lord of hosts, the God of the armies of Israel, whom you have taunted. This day the Lord will deliver you up into my hands, and I will strike you down and remove your head from you."

*As Goliath approached David, David grabbed a stone from his bag and slung it at Goliath, striking his forehead and killing him. No hesitation whatsoever. He knew God would deliver him and his people. He put total trust in God. He had total confidence God would help him. That, my friend, is someone, who despite great obstacles, overcomes the adversary and wins the battle. **I want that kind of faith in my life. How about you?***

QUESTIONS

7. **What is your Goliath? What is it that completely overwhelms you?**

_____

_____

_____

_____

_____

8. **What helps you when you can't move forward? Is it a Bible verse? Is it help from a friend? Read II Corinthians 12:9-10. What encourages you from these verses?**

_____

_____

_____

_____

_____

9. **Give an example of overcoming something monumental in your life. What or who helped you through that obstacle?**

_____

_____

_____

_____

_____

10. *Do you put your trust in God, knowing that He will help you? Read Psalm 56:3, Proverbs 3:5-6, and Isaiah 12:2. What do they tell you?*

_____

_____

_____

_____

_____

_____

_____

_____

_____

11. *Are there steps you can take this week that will help you overcome your Goliath? Write down at least 3 steps that will bring you closer to your goal.*

_____

_____

_____

_____

_____

_____

_____

_____

_____

EPISODE 3

A PRECIOUS COMMODITY

Acts 2:37-47

37 Now when they heard this, they were pierced to the heart, and said to Peter and the rest of the apostles, "Brethren, what shall we do?" 38 Peter said to them, "Repent, and each of you be baptized in the name of Jesus Christ for the forgiveness of your sins; and you will receive the gift of the Holy Spirit. 39 For the promise is for you and your children and for all who are far off, as many as the Lord our God will call to Himself." 40 And with many other words he solemnly testified and kept on exhorting them, saying, "Be saved from this perverse generation!" 41 So then, those who had received his word were baptized; and that day there were added about three thousand souls. 42 They were continually devoting themselves to the apostles' teaching and to fellowship, to the breaking of bread and to prayer. 43 Everyone kept feeling a sense of awe; and many wonders and signs were taking place through the apostles. 44 And all those who had believed were together and had all things in common; 45 and they began selling their property and possessions and were sharing them with all, as anyone might have need. 46 Day by day continuing with one mind in the temple, and breaking bread from house to house, they were taking their meals together with gladness and sincerity of heart, 47 praising God and having favor with all the people. And the Lord was adding to their number day by day those who were being saved.

Hospitality has always been on my heart. Every aspect of it. A lot of that stems from my growing up years. My family was struggling and we needed help. I would always wish somehow someone would come help us. As an adult I knew God wanted us to all be involved with each other's lives enough for us to see each other's needs. The ingathering in Acts 2:37-47 became so important to me. An ingathering is a time of harvest when you bring everything together. This time near Pentecost was a gathering of new believers. These new first century Christians were spending time together every day. They knew one another's needs. Outsiders could see the love they had for each other and the Lord was adding to their numbers daily. **How great is that?!**

In this video I share a testimony from BOLD. I had asked a missionary couple to write a testimony for my book thinking they would share about their bravery working in a dangerous part of the world. But that is not what they sent me. They share about meeting the needs of the saints. They tell how their parents always opened their homes to others and met people's needs. At first I wasn't sure what to think. Then I realized God gave me their testimony to use as an encouragement to be intentional and to take steps to meet the needs of others.

As believers we need to purposefully think of how we can help that person down the street or the relative that seems discouraged. We need to think each week, who can I help?

SO, dear friends, what is your plan?

QUESTIONS

1. **Read Acts chapter 2. How does this passage encourage you? How are you showing Christ's love to others around you?**

_____

_____

_____

_____

2. **Read Psalm 72:12-13. How can you be a helper to those in need? Has the Lord given you compassion for the poor and needy? Add this to your memory verses. If you don't have notecards or a system for scripture memorization, now may be a good time to start. I have to physically have cards on a ring. I am a visual learner. Choose what is best for you.**

_____

_____

_____

3. **Are you observant to the needs around you? What needs do you see right now? Are you ready and willing to boldly offer your time to others?**

_____

_____

_____

_____

4. **Pray for God to give you a heart of compassion. Maybe there is someone crossing your path often but they are not your favorite person.**

    a. Start praying for them. Also pray for yourself to have God's eyes.

    b. Reach out to them and see what is going on with them; you may discover a need you can help with.

    c. Take action.

5. **Make a list of five people who you can reach out to this week, even if it's just a text, a note to them or a short phone call.**

_____

_____

_____

_____

_____

EPISODE 4

BEARING FRUIT

Galatians 5

16 But I say, walk by the Spirit, and you will not carry out the desire of the flesh. 17 For the desire of the flesh is against the Spirit, and the Spirit against the flesh; for these are in opposition to one another, in order to keep you from doing whatever you want. 18 But if you are led by the Spirit, you are not under the Law. 19 Now the deeds of the flesh are evident, which are: sexual immorality, impurity, indecent behavior, 20 idolatry, witchcraft, hostilities, strife, jealousy, outbursts of anger, selfish ambition, dissensions, factions, 21 envy, drunkenness, carousing, and things like these, of which I forewarn you, just as I have forewarned you, that those who practice such things will not inherit the kingdom of God. 22 But the fruit of the Spirit is love, joy, peace, patience, kindness, goodness, faithfulness, 23 gentleness, self-control; against such things there is no law. 24 Now those who belong to Christ Jesus crucified the flesh with its passions and desires.

As a believer we always hear about the "fruit of the spirit", so much so that it almost sounds like a trite expression. But shame on me for thinking that, because no scripture should ever seem trite. It should seem fresh. God teaches us new things all the time no matter how many times we hear a passage. God wants us to grow in godliness and Christian character. It involves love and purity and a deep fervent love for God.

Spiritual growth is usually shown when we start to crave God's Word. And it is displayed to others by them being able to see certain traits in our lives such as love, patience, kindness. How do we obtain this kind of growth? **Let's take a look at some passages that will give us insight.**

QUESTIONS

1. Read Colossians 1:9-10. How does this passage inspire you to walk worthy? What does this passage say is the result of walking worthy?

\
\
\
\
\

2. John 15:1-5 describes how our relationship with Jesus is like a branch to the vine. According to these verses, where does the ability to bear fruit come from?

\
\
\
\
\

3. Read 1 Peter 2:1-3. What causes us to grow in our Christian life?

\
\
\
\

4. *Galatians 5 is the prime passage people look to for fruit of the spirit. Take a look at verses 16-24 at the top of this chapter. Paul begins by telling the Galatians to walk in the spirit and the flesh won't overtake them. Why is this?*

_____

_____

_____

5. *Then in verse 22 we get "the list":*

❖ **Love, joy, and peace** give us an inner well-being or inner calm which comes from our relationship with God.

❖ **Long-suffering** is the result of withstanding a continuous difficulty with God's help.

❖ **Kindness** is a tender concern for other people.

❖ **Goodness** is moral excellence, being above reproach or accusation.

❖ **Faithfulness** is being loyal and trustworthy.

❖ **Gentleness** is being humble in spirit.

❖ **Self-control** is all about restraint.

6. *That is quite a list. Sometimes I think the focus is on the first three. And they are so very important, but the others go deep into our hearts. As the list grows, it gets more convicting. I think that is why self-control is last. Look at each of these and write down how you can work on these traits in your own life.*

_____

_____

_____

_____

7. *Prayer helps you to bear fruit. Try using ACTS when you pray. Start with adoration, confession and thanksgiving before making requests of God. Write out a short prayer using "ACTS" regarding the fruits of the spirit.*

❖ **Adoration** - Praise God for who He is and His character traits

❖ **Confession** - Acknowledge your sinful thoughts and behavior to God

❖ **Thanksgiving** - Thank God for what he has done in your life

❖ **Supplication** - Ask God to help in specific situations and circumstances

_____

_____

_____

_____

_____

_____

_____

_____

_____

_____

_____

EPISODE 5

WHAT'S IN FRONT OF YOU?

1 Samuel 25:3, 18-19

> *3 Now the man's name was Nabal, and his wife's name was Abigail. And the woman was intelligent and beautiful in appearance, but the man was harsh and evil in his dealings, and he was a Calebite,*

> *18 Then Abigail hurried and took two hundred loaves of bread and two jugs of wine, and five sheep already prepared and five measures of roasted grain, and a hundred cakes of raisins and two hundred cakes of figs, and she loaded them on donkeys. 19 Then she said to her young men, "Go on ahead of me; behold, I am coming after you." But she did not tell her husband Nabal.*

What are the resources you have in front of you to help you to mature and stay focused on meeting each other's needs? In the last lesson, we discussed the fruit in our lives. So let's put feet to our kindness and love, and create action.

In 1 Samuel we see the story of Nabal's wife, Abigail. This is a favorite of mine. Nabal was not a nice man. He had wronged David and his men. When Abigail heard of this, knowing that David would come to kill her husband and her people, she acted quickly and problem-solved the situation. She showed wisdom and discernment in what she said to King David and in doing so she rescued her people. Despite her husband's evil, David had great respect for Abigail and showed mercy and compassion to her and her people.

I love this story because it is such a great example of the ability to assess a situation quickly and make a plan in an emergency while seeking good for others.

QUESTIONS

1. **Read 1 Samuel 25:18-19. Go ahead and read the entire chapter. Abigail is a woman who takes action quickly and efficiently. What was the problem? And how did she solve it?**

_____

_____

_____

_____

2. **In what ways could you be more efficient so you would be ready on a moment's notice to help someone if they phoned you with a problem or even came to your house needing help?**

_____

_____

_____

_____

3. What resources do you have that you can use to meet the needs of others?

_____

_____

_____

_____

_____

4. In the video for this lesson I share my testimony of growing up with a widowed mom and sister on our farm with no income. I longed for someone to come help us. Do you have someone you need to check on? Someone who you have not heard from for a while, or perhaps a neighbor you always thought about helping? Take this opportunity right now while it is fresh in your mind to check on someone today.

_____

_____

_____

_____

5. Pray that God would give you the ability to discern the needs of others, and show you the wisdom to use the resources He has given you to meet those needs.

_____

_____

_____

_____

_____

EPISODE 6

THE MISSING INGREDIENT

Deuteronomy 15

1 At the end of every seven years you shall grant a release of debts. 2 And this is the regulation for the release of debts: every creditor is to forgive what he has loaned to his neighbor; he shall not require it of his neighbor and his brother, because the Lord's release has been proclaimed. 3 From a foreigner you may require it, but your hand shall forgive whatever of yours is with your brother. 4 However, there will be no poor among you, since the Lord will certainly bless you in the land which the Lord your God is giving you as an inheritance to possess, 5 if only you listen obediently to the voice of the Lord your God, to follow carefully all this command-ment which I am commanding you today. 6 For the Lord your God will have blessed you just as He has promised you, and you will lend to many nations, but you will not borrow; and you will rule over many nations, but they will not rule over you.

7 If there is a poor person among you, one of your brothers, in any of your towns in your land which the Lord your God is giving you, you shall not harden your heart, nor close your hand from your poor brother; 8 but you shall fully open your hand to him, and generously lend him enough for his need in whatever he lacks. 9 Be careful that there is no mean-spirited thought in your heart, such as, 'The seventh year, the year of release of debts, is near,' and your eye is malicious toward your poor brother, and you give him nothing; then he may cry out to the Lord against you, and it will be a sin in you. 10 You shall generously give to him, and your heart shall not be grudging when you give to him, because for this thing the Lord your God will bless you in all your work, and in all your undertakings. 11 For the poor will not cease to exist in the land; therefore I am commanding you, saying, 'You shall fully open your hand to your brother, to your needy and poor in your land.'

12 If your fellow countryman, a Hebrew man or woman, is sold to you, then he shall serve you for six years, but in the seventh year you shall set him free. 13 And when you set him free, you shall not *send him away empty-handed.* **14** *You shall give generously to him from your flock, your threshing floor, and from your wine vat; you shall give to him as the Lord your God has blessed you.* **15** *And you are to remember that you were a slave in the land of Egypt, and the Lord your God redeemed you; therefore I am commanding this of you today.* **16** *But it shall come about, if he says to you, 'I will not leave you,' because he loves you and your household, since he is doing well with you,* **17** *then you shall take an awl and pierce it through his ear into the door, and he shall be your servant permanently. You shall also do the same to your female slave.**

*18** *It shall not seem difficult for you when you set him free, because he has given you six years with double the service of a hired worker; so the Lord your God will bless you in whatever you do.*

*19** *You shall consecrate to the Lord your God all the firstborn males that are born in your herd and in your flock; you shall not work with the firstborn of your herd, nor shear the firstborn of your flock.* **20** *You and your household shall eat it every year before the Lord your God in the place which the Lord chooses.* **21** *But if it has any impairment, such as a limp, or blindness, or any serious impairment, you shall not sacrifice it to the Lord your God.* **22** *You shall eat it within your gates; the unclean and the* *clean alike may eat it, as a gazelle or a deer. 23 Only you shall not eat its blood; you are to pour it out on the ground like water.*

1 John 3:17

17 But whoever has worldly goods and sees his brother or sister in need, and closes his heart against him, how does the love of God remain in him?

What motivates you to reach out to your neighbor? When we think of compassion, it's not just for those we know but sometimes it's about those we may not know at all. Compassion is defined as the "sympathetic pity or concern for the sufferings or misfortunes of others"

.

The Old Testament has become dearer to my heart as I have gotten older. So many believers know the New Testament backwards and forwards but seldom study the Old Testament. Years ago I was told by someone that the Old Testament was so important and that Deuteronomy was the most important book in the Bible. Definitely a big claim. I disagreed then, but through the years I have totally come to understand his point. It describes our holy, righteous God and how we are to live. It is quoted 40 times in the New Testament. It tells us what we can do to obey and how we can live a righteous life.

In this lesson we are focusing on Deuteronomy chapter 15. It was the sabbatical year in Israel. Every seventh year if you could not grow crops and were not able to pay your debts, they would be canceled. The attitude of the Israelites toward the poor was to be warm and generous. The poor were given what was necessary to meet their needs even if they were never able to repay.

We need to consider our perspective on those less fortunate.

QUESTIONS

1. **Read Deuteronomy 15. What from this passage might motivate you to reach out to others?**

_____

_____

_____

_____

_____

_____

2. **What has been your view of the poor? Reread Deuteronomy 15:10-11. This passage tells us there will always be poor in the land. Does this impact your opinion of the needy? How does this encourage you to continue to have compassion?**

_____

_____

_____

_____

3. **Do you have a hard time reaching out to people you do not know? What are ways that may help you be more bold?**

_____

_____

_____

_____

_____

4. What is true compassion to you? What example have you seen of this in your life? Have you seen someone demonstrate this to someone else or to you?

_____

_____

_____

_____

_____

5. List five attributes of God. How does understanding who God is change your perception of the poor or needy?

_____

_____

_____

_____

_____

6. Read 1 John 3:17. Is your heart ready to help someone? What are ways you can prepare your heart? How can you pray to meet the needs of others? Who can you help this month?

_____

_____

_____

_____

EPISODE 7

DAY CHALLENGE

What if Mary
Had been too frightened of the unknown,
Too worried of what people would say and think,
To yield to God's will to bear His Son?

What if Joseph
Had not believed the angel in his dream,
Had not believed the child Mary carried was Holy,
And had chosen instead to divorce her?

What if the shepherds
Had been too preoccupied watching their sheep,
Too busy calculating what they would get for them,
To hear what the angels had to say?

What if the magi
Had been too engrossed gaining more knowledge,
Too stretched and stressed with their lecture tours,
To make the trip to Bethlehem?

What if today we
Are too busy and focused on other things
We miss the Good News that Christ our Savior
Has been born and is coming again?

By: Unknown

Sometimes we need to challenge ourselves. Light a fire under our faith. Push ourselves out of our comfort zone to serve and love people for Christ. Earlier this year I challenged my viewers to do a 30 Day Challenge with me. We had a schedule of what to do each day and each task was pretty quick and easy. We read Scripture, memorized verses, prayed, did service projects, and put effort into relationships. It was amazing to see what people were able to do and accomplish and how this helped them gain confidence to go out of their comfort zone.

QUESTIONS

1. **What are your ideas on how to go out of your comfort zone to love and serve people?**

_____

_____

_____

2. **Which of these tasks would be easiest for you? Which would be hardest? Why?**

_____

_____

_____

3. **What actions will you take?**

_____

_____

_____

4. *What are your thoughts on the previous poem? Are you too busy? Too frightened? Too preoccupied? Or too engrossed in something else to hear what God wants you to do?*

_____

_____

_____

5. *This is the challenge my LIVE BOLDLY Facebook group did last January. You could use a similar format or make up your own.*

30 Day Challenge – January 2022

Legend:
- Scripture to Read
- Mark/Memorize
- Take Action
- Worship
- Talk to God/Pray
- Family and Friends
- Service

Sunday	Monday	Tuesday	Wednesday	Thursday	Friday	Saturday
						1 ❏ Help someone with a chore
2 ❏ Read Col 3:12-17	**3** ❏ Memorize Col 3:12	**4** ❏ Send encouraging note	**5** ❏ Worship through Prayer	**6** ❏ Pray for 5 fellow believers	**7** ❏ Connect with a family member	**8** ❏ Take a meal to someone
9 ❏ Read Matt 9:36-38	**10** ❏ Circle the word "love" in 1 John	**11** ❏ Meet a new neighbor	**12** ❏ Worship through Nature	**13** ❏ Prayer of adoration to God	**14** ❏ Get together with a friend	**15** ❏ Visit a shut-in
16 ❏ Read Rom 12	**17** ❏ Memorize Rom 12:13	**18** ❏ Give to an unlikely recipient	**19** ❏ Worship through Song	**20** ❏ Pray for 5 areas of thankfulness	**21** ❏ Restore a lost relationship	**22** ❏ Take a meal to someone
23 ❏ Read Deut 15	**24** ❏ Mark each "bless", "blessing" in Deut 15	**25** ❏ Share your testimony w/ someone	**26** ❏ Worship through Giving	**27** ❏ Prayer of Confession	**28** ❏ Get together with a friend	**29** ❏ Choose an act of service
30 ❏ Read Heb 13	**31** ❏ Memorize Heb 13:16					

EPISODE 8

PUT ON A HEART OF COMPASSION

Colossians 3:12-17

12 So, as those who have been chosen of God, holy and beloved, put on a heart of compassion, kindness, humility, gentleness, and patience; 13 bearing with one another, and forgiving each other, whoever has a complaint against anyone; just as the Lord forgave you, so must you do also. 14 In addition to all these things put on love, which is the perfect bond of unity. 15 Let the peace of Christ, to which you were indeed called in one body, rule in your hearts; and be thankful. 16 Let the word of Christ richly dwell within you, with all wisdom teaching and admonishing one another with psalms, hymns, and spiritual songs, singing with thankfulness in your hearts to God. 17 Whatever you do in word or deed, do everything in the name of the Lord Jesus, giving thanks through Him to God the Father.

I love the third chapter of Colossians. As a matter of fact, that is why my team started Colossians 3:12 ministries.

If we are to be doers of the Word and purposeful in what we do, we must have compassion. In this episode I share a bit about why I wrote my first book, "Not Really a Princess". Trials my family went through were difficult. Because of these trials, I wished someone would help us. Through the years more and more happened, and people kept saying, "someone needs to write about this", so I did. I thought, "how can my story encourage someone else?" Being aware of unmet needs and the desire to encourage people to meet those needs, I wrote my second book, "It's Not About the Pie: A Fresh Look at Hospitality", and we created Colossians 3:12 Ministries.

For some background on this passage, it is important to note that Paul was in prison in Rome. Epaphras went to him because the people at the church at Colossae were struggling and he was concerned for them. He needed Paul's insight on how to help them. As a result, Paul wrote a letter to the church. He told them what not to do and what they should do. It is inspiring for us all.

QUESTIONS

1. **Read Colossians 3:12-17. What does it mean to you to be "chosen by God"?**

_____

_____

_____

2. God wants us to "put on" a heart of compassion. Compassion is caring and feeling deeply for someone who is having difficulties, plus acting on that feeling. Think of someone you have compassion for. What action can you take to put "legs to your caring"?

_____

_____

_____

3. Many of the ideas in our 30 Day Challenge are action items where we show compassion, kindness, humility, meekness and patience. Which of these attributes can you see evidenced in your life? Ask a friend or family member which of these traits they see in you.

_____

_____

_____

4. Be intentional in having and showing a heart of compassion. We all get busy with our own lives and are tired at the end of a long day. Pray for opportunities to show compassion to others today.

_____

_____

5. Do you believe fully that God can use you? The more you study His Word the more you begin to forget about yourself and your insecurities and trust His plan.

_____

_____

6. Read Matthew 5:16 and Philippians 2:4. In what ways do you believe God can use you to show kindness and compassion to others?

_____

_____

_____

EPISODE 9

JESUS MOVED WITH COMPASSION

Matthew 9:35-38

> *35 Jesus was going through all the cities and villages, teaching in their synagogues and proclaiming the gospel of the kingdom, and healing every disease and every sickness. 36 Seeing the crowds, He felt compassion for them, because they were distressed and downcast, like sheep without a shepherd. 37 Then He said to His disciples, "The harvest is plentiful, but the workers are few. 38 Therefore, plead with the Lord of the harvest to send out workers into His harvest."*

Joshua 24:15

> *15 But if it is disagreeable in your sight to serve the Lord, choose for yourselves today whom you will serve: whether the gods which your fathers served, which were beyond the Euphrates River, or the gods of the Amorites in whose land you are living; but as for me and my house, we will serve the Lord.*

2 Timothy 4:2-4

> *2 preach the word; be ready in season and out of season; correct, rebuke, and exhort, with great patience*

and instruction. 3 For the time will come when they will not tolerate sound doctrine; but wanting to have their ears tickled, they will accumulate for themselves teachers in accordance with their own desires, 4 and they will turn their ears away from the truth and will turn aside to myths.

As I was reviewing this video episode and looking at my notes, I kept thinking about how the TV series, "The Chosen" has brought the gospels to life for so many people. Some have said that in print the gospels are black and white but watching this makes them in color. That is a good way to think about it. Don't get me wrong, Scripture is not lacking, but I never really thought of what they had to eat or that they had to chop firewood or find a place to sleep at night. I also like the fact that the disciples and Jesus joke with each other. It helps you to realize that they are real people.

This brings us to the lesson. In one of "The Chosen" episodes, Jesus is healing a long line of people all day - standing in the heat. The disciples and women who help Him are back at camp eating dinner and getting ready for bed. Some of them are complaining that Jesus is always gone, and then He comes into the camp - totally exhausted. They tell him there is dinner for him but He says He just needs rest. His feet are swollen and He heads straight to His tent. So many times Jesus was swarmed with people, but He was moved with compassion and would minister no matter how tired He was. We see Jesus' humanity. He is fully God but also fully human.

Do you feel compassion for those around you? Let's share some scripture and thoughts.

QUESTIONS

1. Read 2 Timothy 1:7. How do you respond to this scripture? Define - timid, discipline

2. Read Matthew 9. Jesus is asking for our help. How do your prayers reflect your desire for opportunities to serve God and share the gospel with others?

3. Memorize Joshua 24:15. What does it mean to you to "serve the Lord"? What are things you do to serve the Lord?

4. Are you working on the 30 Day Challenge? Even if you are not doing the entire thing, I hope you are encouraged to DAILY think of ways to share the gospel and help others. Write down three ways you can serve others this month.

5. Read II Timothy 4:2-4. Are you ready to share your faith with someone? Think of a few situations where it is easy to share your faith. What makes it easy? Now think of the reasons it is hard to share your faith. Pray that the Lord would help you overcome these obstacles.

EPISODE 10
SERVING THE SAINTS

Romans 12:1-2

> *1 Therefore I urge you, brothers and sisters, by the mercies of God, to present your bodies as a living and holy sacrifice, acceptable to God, which is your spiritual service of worship. 2 And do not be conformed to this world, but be transformed by the renewing of your mind, so that you may prove what the will of God is, that which is good and acceptable and perfect.*

1 Peter 4:9

> *9 Be hospitable to one another without complaint.*

As I shared in the video, the first time I went into a Bible-believing church, they were memorizing Romans 12:1-2 together as a congregation. I had briefly gone to a church where you didn't bring your Bible, so this was a shocker. These verses became important to me. God's grace transforms us, and as that happens we become more aware of ways to share our lives with others, meet their needs, and share our faith.

In verse 13 of Romans 12, Paul tells us to "contribute to the needs of the saints, practice hospitality". This is not a casual instruction but a direct request imploring believers to help others. ***Make it happen. These verses are keys to how we live our life as a believer.***

QUESTIONS

1. **Read Romans 12:1-13. God is transforming you. He is taking away your former ways of life and placing new traits in you as you grow. From this passage, what ways do you see yourself growing and serving?**

_____

_____

_____

_____

_____

2. **In 1 Peter 4:9 it says we are to be hospitable without grumbling. I think oftentimes we grow weary of doing good; we drag our feet instead of jumping in to help. In Greek this phrase actually means to "go at a word", like being instantly ready to go and help. I have had trouble with this: I was recently asked to work in the 2's and 3's in Sunday School. This is not my thing (wish I could give you a grimace emoji). I had been a substitute teacher for years and was scared of kids under 8. I have worked in kids ministry for years in our AWANA program - but 2's and 3's?! My first thought was...uh...no. But the person asking is very dear to me, so I said "yes". I definitely dragged my feet with this. Guess what? It was great. No problems. Sometimes there is a need and we just are supposed to help, whether it is in our wheelhouse or not. Share an example of when you have dropped everything to help someone.**

_____

_____

_____

_____

3. What resources/skills do you have that you can share with others? Your time, a ride, food? The ability to do things like use a computer, budget finances, or fix a car? Remember, being generous is a lifestyle. What in your life can be used to assist others?

_____

_____

_____

_____

_____

4. Read 2 Corinthians 9:6-8. God gives us "all sufficiency", everything we need to help others. He also gives us the inner joy to be cheerful about it. What have you "purposed in your heart" to do this week? In what ways will you reach out to a neighbor or coworker this week?

_____

_____

_____

_____

_____

5. How has God blessed you for giving cheerfully to others?

_____

_____

_____

_____

EPISODE 11

FREELY OPENING YOUR HAND TO OTHERS

Deuteronomy 15:7-8, 10-11

7 If there is a poor person among you, one of your brothers, in any of your towns in your land which the Lord your God is giving you, you shall not harden your heart, nor close your hand from your poor brother; 8 but you shall fully open your hand to him, and generously lend him enough for his need in whatever he lacks. 10 You shall generously give to him, and your heart shall not be grudging when you give to him, because for this thing the Lord your God will bless you in all your work, and in all your undertakings. 11 For the poor will not cease to exist in the land; therefore I am command-ing you, saying, 'You shall fully open your hand to your brother, to your needy and poor in your land.'

Galatians 2:10

10 They only asked us to remember the poor—the very thing I also was eager to do.

Ephesians 4:28

28 The one who steals must no longer steal; but rather he must

labor, producing with his own hands what is good, so that he
will have something to share with the one who has need.

James 2:14-17

14 What use is it, my brothers and sisters, if some-
one says he has faith, but he has no works? Can that
faith save him? 15 If a brother or sister is without
clothing and in need of daily food, 16 and one of
you says to them, "Go in peace, be warmed and be
filled," yet you do not give them what is necessary
for their body, what use is that? 17 In the same way,
faith also, if it has no works, is dead, being by itself.

For about a decade now, Deuteronomy has been a favorite passage of mine. Maybe it's because I grew up on a
farm and there wasn't a lot extra, and after my dad passed
there was less. Funny how I didn't really think it mattered
a lot until my teen years when the needs grew. So, truth-
fully, it REALLY annoys me when people *dismiss the needs*
of poor people, and think they should just go get a job,
or assume they mismanaged their life so it is their fault
that they have difficulties, or that we don't need to help
them....Just being truthful.

Deuteronomy 15:11 says, "The poor will not cease to
be in the land." So true. I am not saying that there aren't
people who are lazy and maybe expect help. There will
always be those too. Although…they need Jesus too. That's
a whole other conversation. **Let's address what we are**
supposed to do.

QUESTIONS

1. **Read Deuteronomy 15. This chapter has to do with the sabbatical year when the people were supposed to forgive debts of people who owed them. So how does this apply to us? Just like the entire Bible, it is there for a reason. Reread verses 7 & 8 and 10 & 11.** *"Be careful that there is not a mean spirited thought in your heart."* **Hmmm, I do believe this applies to our attitude. What else do you glean from this passage? List three truths.**

_____

_____

_____

_____

_____

2. **Read Galatians 2:10. Paul is referring to the growing ranks of believers moving in and staying in Jerusalem. The local believers had shared what they had but were being stretched thin. How does this encourage us?**

_____

_____

_____

_____

_____

_____

3. **Ephesians 4:8 is a verse often taught to children but sometimes they are taught just the first half of the verse. However, the verse continues to tell us to work so we may have something to share with others. What are some ways we can share something we have this week with someone in need?**

_____

_____

_____

_____

_____

_____

4. **James 2 is all about faith. Is our faith true and real or not? Do we feel compassion or not? Do we want to share or not? Read this chapter and share your thoughts on what your role may be.**

_____

_____

_____

_____

_____

5. **Write down your testimony in a short paragraph. Keep it short so it is easy to remember, and easy to share with others. Include what Jesus did for you and how that has changed or helped you.**

_____

_____

_____

_____

EPISODE 12

DO NOT NEGLECT DOING GOOD AND SHARING WITH OTHERS

Hebrews 13

1 Let love of the brothers and sisters continue. 2 Do not neglect hospitality to strangers, for by this some have entertained angels without knowing it. 3 Remember the prisoners, as though in prison with them, and those who are badly treated, since you yourselves also are in the body. 4 Marriage is to be held in honor among all, and the marriage bed is to be undefiled; for God will judge the sexually immoral and adulterers. 5 Make sure that your character is free from the love of money, being content with what you have; for He Himself has said, "I will never desert you, nor will I ever abandon you," 6 so that we confidently say,

"The Lord is my helper, I will not be afraid.

What will man do to me?"

7 Remember those who led you, who spoke the word of God to you; and considering the result of their way of life, imitate their faith. 8 Jesus Christ is the same yesterday and today, and forever. 9 Do not be misled by varied and strange teachings; for it is good for the heart to be strengthened by grace, not by foods, through which those who were so occupied were not benefited. 10 We have an altar from which those who serve the tabernacle have no right to eat. 11 For the bodies of those animals whose blood is brought into the Holy Place by the high priest as an offering for sin are burned outside the camp. 12 Therefore Jesus also suffered outside the gate, that He might sanctify the people through His own blood. 13 So then, let us go out to Him outside the camp, bearing His reproach. 14 For here we do not have a lasting city, but we are seeking the city which is to come. 15 Through Him then, let's continually offer up a sacrifice of praise to God, that is, the fruit of lips praising His name. 16 And do not neglect doing good and sharing, for with such sacrifices God is pleased. 17 Obey your leaders and submit to them—for they keep watch over your souls as those who will give an account—so that they may do this with joy, not groaning; for this would be unhelpful for you. 18 Pray for us, for we are sure that we have a good conscience, desiring to conduct ourselves honorably in all things. 19 And I urge you all the more to do this, so that I may be restored to you more quickly. 20 Now may the God of peace, who brought up from the dead the great Shepherd of the sheep through the blood of the eternal covenant, that is, Jesus our Lord, 21 equip you in every good thing to do His will, working in us that which is pleasing in His sight, through Jesus Christ, to whom be the glory forever and ever. Amen. 22 But I urge you, brothers and sisters, listen patiently to this word of exhortation, for I have written to you briefly. 23 Know that our brother Timothy has been released, with whom, if he comes soon, I will see you. 24 Greet all of your leaders and all the saints. Those from Italy greet you. 25 Grace be with you all.

Proverbs 22:9

9 One who is generous will be blessed, Because he gives some of his food to the poor.

Proverbs 31:20

20 She extends her hand to the poor, And she stretches out her hands to the needy.

Hebrews 13 is a favorite passage for many people. It is full of Christian principles for our daily lives. Our relationship with Christ overflows into all we do - not just to our brothers and sisters in Christ but also to non-believers. People who have encouraged and mentored us are great examples to us. Being a disciple is all about multiplication. We learn and grow from those who are strong in their faith and then we share with others. I love verse 7, "Remember those who led you, who spoke the word of God to you, and considering the result of life, imitate their faith". That is something I would wish for you.

Later in the passage in verse 15-16 it says, "Through Him then, let us continually offer up a sacrifice of praise to God, that is, the fruit of lips praising His name. And do not neglect doing good and sharing, for with such sacrifices God is pleased." We are praising God by doing good and sharing with others. What a great thing.

> **Each one of you has your own gift: be who you are, who God made you to be. You don't have to do everything. Share those gifts with others.**

QUESTIONS

1. **Read Hebrews 13. Underline key phrases that you can focus on this week.**

_____

_____

_____

2. **Read Proverbs 22:9. What are three ways you can be generous? Think of specific things you can do and take action! Remember, the little ways you show kindness - like taking someone's grocery cart back for them - are just as important as a larger gesture.**

_____

_____

_____

3. *Read Habakkuk 3:18-19. Who gives us the strength we need when we shrink back from doing good and sharing with others?*

_____

_____

_____

_____

_____

4. *Reread Hebrews 13:7. Think of a person who has been an example of faith to you. How have you tried to imitate or emulate them? Do you have someone who looks to you as an example of a faithful Christian?*

_____

_____

_____

_____

_____

5. *Proverbs 31:20 tells us,* "she opens her hand to the poor and extends her hand to the needy". **How does this verse encourage you? What is another verse you can find on this subject?**

_____

_____

_____

_____

EPISODE 13

THE CITY ON A HILL

1 Peter 2: 9-12

9 But you are a chosen people, a royal priesthood, a holy nation, a people for God's own possession, so that you may proclaim the excellencies of Him who has called you out of darkness into His marvelous light; 10 for you once were not a people, but now you are the people of God; you had not received mercy, but now you have received mercy. 11 Beloved, I urge you as foreigners and strangers to abstain from fleshly lusts, which wage war against the soul. 12 Keep your behavior excellent among the Gentiles, so that in the thing in which they slander you as evildoers, they may because of your good deeds, as they observe them, glorify God on the day of visitation.

Matthew 5:1-11

1 Now when Jesus saw the crowds, He went up on the mountain; and after He sat down, His disciples came to Him. 2 And He opened His mouth and began to teach them, saying, 3 "Blessed are the

poor in spirit, for theirs is the kingdom of heaven.
4 "Blessed are those who mourn, for they will be
comforted. 5 "Blessed are the gentle, for they will
inherit the earth. 6 "Blessed are those who hunger
and thirst for righteousness, for they will be satis-
fied. 7 "Blessed are the merciful, for they will receive
mercy. 8 "Blessed are the pure in heart, for they will
see God. 9 "Blessed are the peacemakers, for they
will be called sons of God. 10 "Blessed are those who
have been persecuted for the sake of righteousness,
for theirs is the kingdom of heaven. 11 "Blessed
are you when people insult you and persecute you,
and falsely say all kinds of evil against you because
of Me. 12 Rejoice and be glad, for your reward in
heaven is great; for in this same way they persecut-
ed the prophets who were before you.

I have always loved the Sermon on the Mount. Those chapters in Matthew have always inspired me. They are so incredibly full of amazing truths. Having watched the second season of "The Chosen", I have realized what an extreme undertaking that day was for everyone. Not just all that Jesus needed to do to be able to teach for so long to thousands of people, but the disciples had to find the place and build a stage etc. with hardly any money. As the disciples helped prepare, I am sure they did not quite know what to expect. Of course, we don't know all the things they did to prepare, but watching the video series has made me do some thinking.

Jesus was hoping to inspire believers to grow in their faith and to show unbelievers the way. This episode stems from Matthew 5:14-16, "You are the light of the world. A city set on a hill cannot be hidden, nor do people light a lamp and put it under a basket, but on the lampstand, and it gives light to all who are in the house. Your light must shine before people in such a way that they may see your good works, and glorify your Father who is in heaven."

This sermon was an opportunity for Jesus's disciples to begin to see the purpose of following Christ. They were part of the biggest thing in history; common men chosen to be a part of the greatest thing of all time.

QUESTIONS

1. **Read Matthew 5-7. Outline the different sections.**

_____

_____

_____

_____

_____

2. **The word "Blessed" means, "happy, fortunate, blissful". The world does not think much about the attitudes and characteristics mentioned in Matthew 5:1-11. Most people would have a different list of things that would make them "happy". . Jesus gives us a description of the characteristics of true faith, true happiness. Which ones do you associate with the most?**

_____

_____

_____

_____

_____

_____

3. **Read 1 Peter 2:9-12. Why is it important for us to live righteous lives?**

_____

_____

_____

_____

_____

_____

4. **What does it mean for us to be a light to the world? Can you give examples from Scripture?**

_____

_____

_____

_____

_____

_____

5. **If others can't see your light, they are not going to see Christ in us. What people, or groups of people, are watching you as you shine your light. Can they see the love of God in you by the good things you do? Are you hiding your light? If so, why?**

_____

_____

_____

_____

_____

_____

EPISODE 14

SHARING A LIFE OF FAITH

2 Timothy 2:2

> 2 *The things which you have heard from me in the presence of many witnesses, entrust these to faithful people who will be able to teach others also.*

Proverbs 27:17

> 17 *As iron sharpens iron, So one person sharpens another.*

1 Thessalonians 2:8

> 8 *in the same way we had a fond affection for you and were delighted to share with you not only the gospel of God, but also our own lives, because you had become very dear to us.*

Mentoring is all about sharing life with people. How can we minister to others if we don't listen, or spend time, or learn about them? And I am not just talking about doing a Bible study with someone, but hanging out with them so they know how much you really care no matter who they are or what they have going on in their life.

> *Do you know where they work or go to school? Do you know their faith history? These things give us insight into their lives.*

I read through the Apostle Paul's books and see how he always was with other men to teach and share ministry with them, like when he lived in Corinth for 1 ½ years with Aquila and Priscilla. They did life together. They were tentmakers together, and they shared in having the house church ministry. Corinth was a corrupt place, more than some other places he had been on that journey, but he stayed there longer than any other place. He was building something valuable.

He also had a close relationship with Timothy. When Paul knew his time on earth was drawing to a close, it was Timothy he wanted to come to him.

These are important things to remember. You are teaching others to grow in their faith so they in turn can teach someone else…multiplication.

QUESTIONS

1. **Read 2 Timothy 2:2, Proverbs 27:17, and 1 Thessalonians 2:8. What do these verses have in common? What is the key idea?**

_____

_____

_____

_____

_____

2. **List five things you can do in a discipler role to encourage someone in their faith.**

_____

_____

_____

3. **Read Psalm 71:18, Proverbs 22:6, and Titus 2:3-4. These verses refaer to family. What are ways you can minister to specific people in your family? Is there someone you have been praying for that you could reach out to this week?**

_____

_____

_____

4. **In order to share your faith with others, you need to be strong in your own faith. Read John 14:26 and Proverbs 13:20. What do these verses tell you?**

_____

_____

_____

5. **Hebrews 13:7 is a verse we have used a few times in our series. Why? Because it wraps all this up in a nutshell.** "Remember those who led you, who spoke the word of God to you; and considering the result of their conduct, **imitate their faith." List three things in your life of faith that another person can imitate.**

_____

_____

_____

_____

EPISODE 15

WORLD CHANGING DISCIPLES

John 21:15-17

15 Now when they had finished breakfast, Jesus said to Simon Peter, "Simon, son of John, do you love Me more than these?" He said to Him, "Yes, Lord; You know that I love You." He said to him, "Tend My lambs." 16 He said to him again, a second time, "Simon, son of John, do you love Me?" He said to Him, "Yes, Lord; You know that I love You." He said to him, "Shepherd My sheep." 17 He said to him the third time, "Simon, son of John, do you love Me?" Peter was hurt because He said to him the third time, "Do you love Me?" And he said to Him, "Lord, You know all things; You know that I love You." Jesus said to him, "Tend My sheep."

As we wrap up this video series workbook, it is time for the rubber to meet the road. Jesus did not choose scholars or famous men to follow Him. He chose ordinary men. They just needed to be willing. Have you been thinking of someone you could meet with as you have been going through this workbook? Let your light shine. Do not hide your faith. Find someone in your life that lives their own faith and use them as an example in your own life. THEN pass that on to someone else.

> The disciples were world changers. God used them to change the world. Be like them. Learn from them. Study the Word. It is your guidebook. **Be on your knees for God to give you someone to mentor.**

QUESTIONS

1. **Read John 13:15. Jesus is telling us that He has given us examples to follow. Do you have someone in your own life who has been an example for you? Describe the impact he or she had on you.**

2. **Read John 21:15-17. Did you ever wonder why Jesus chose Peter to be the leader of the church? Peter seemed so impulsive and bullheaded, always questioning Jesus. However, he was also the one who was a leader. Someone who questions things and figures things out is usually someone who will get things done. Peter was the one who followed Jesus after his arrest, even denying knowing Him. Jesus knew the good and bad about Peter, yet He chose him to "feed His sheep". He has chosen YOU. What are you doing to "feed His sheep"?**

3. **Here is a list I found online at justdisciple.com, created by Avery Rimilller, but I have added my own comments. The 7 steps to intentional discipleship are:**

   a. Follow first - you can't have an empty cup. You need to be fed too.

   b. Love others - with purpose. Pray for God to give you a deep passion for others to grow.

   c. Get practical - be interested in things they enjoy.

   d. Teach God's Word - it is our toolbox.

   e. Pray together - it honors God and brings healing.

   f. Serve together

   g. Worship together

4. **What are you doing to fulfill each of these steps?**

   _____

   _____

   _____

   _____

   _____

5. **Discipleship is helping others to have a deeper walk with God. What things have you done in a discipleship relationship? Share them with someone else who is wanting to disciple others.**

   _____

   _____

   _____

   _____

   _____

ABOUT THE AUTHOR

Nicki Corinne White has a passion for studying and teaching God's Word. She has been leading Bible studies for many years and discipling young women. She is very involved in her local church with both children's ministry and women's ministry. She has a tender heart for those who are hurting and those who are new to church. Nicki hopes to be an encouragement to those around her lending a listening ear, kind word or a Biblical reminder. She also opens her home to share and serve others through hospitality on a regular basis and believes we are all called to do this. Nicki feels blessed to have been able to use her story and personal experience to encourage others and hopes to expand this ministry through her writing.

Nicki Corinne grew up in Snohomish, Washington, with her mom, dad and sister Lisa. She was adopted at the age of one with her sister Lisa into the Maynard family. Nicki went to college at a small Christian Liberal Arts College in Southern California. She met her husband, Craig, after graduating and was married two years later. They moved to Central California then on to the bay area where they had their first three children. Five years later, they moved to Boise, Idaho where their fourth child was born. Nicki has worked several jobs including teaching, merchandizing, administrative work, and various artist projects. She enjoys spending time outdoors, painting, writing, and spending time with her four children and seven grandkids.

Nicki Corinne has published three books now, "Not Really a Princess", "It's Not About The Pie", and "Bold: Living Intentionally in Today's World". She looks forward to sharing this workbook with you and others in the future to correlate with the video series "LIVE BOLDLY".

CONTACT US

Nicki Corinne White is available for book signings and speaking engagements. To get in touch with her team, please email us or message us through her website.

Email:
nickicorinnewhite@gmail.com

Website:
www.nickicorinne.com

Social Media:
Facebook
Instagram
Twitter

CPSIA information can be obtained
at www.ICGtesting.com
Printed in the USA
JSHW060800160922
30538JS00005B/11